THE GREAT

Sunflower Book

THE GREAT

Sunflower Book

A Guidebook with Recipes

Barbara Flores

Photography by Lois Ellen Frank

Ten Speed Press
Berkeley, California

Also by Barbara Flores
Confusion Is a State of Grace

Ten Speed Press
Post Office Box 7123
Berkeley, California 94707

Distributed in Australia by Tower Books, in Canada by Publishers Group West, in New Zealand by Tandem Press, in South Africa by Real Books, in Southeast Asia by Berkeley Books, and in the United Kingdom and Europe by Airlift Books.

Design by Barbara Flores
Design implemented by Jaime Robles

Photo credits: Bridgeman Art Library, London: 16–17. Chester, Jonathan: inside front and back cover; i; 28, top; 132. Dancer, Daniel: 116–117. Flores, Barbara: 3; 61, top; 102. Kapuler, Kusra: 57, top; 63, top; 68. Kaspar, Susanne: 52–53; 77; 90. Minnesota Historical Society: 10–11; 13. National Sunflower Association: 9, top; 92–93. North Dakota Institute for Regional Studies: 6–7. Vlaun, Scott: vi–vii; x; 15; 38; 39, top; 48, top and bottom; 49, top; 60–61, bottom; 63, bottom; 64–65; 79, top; 80; 88; 95; 96; 110; 115; 118; 121

Pages 11–15 are excerpted from *Buffalo Bird Woman's Garden: Agriculture of the Hidatsa Indians*, as told to Gilbert L. Wilson, reprint edition, St. Paul: Minnesota Historical Society Press, 1987. Reprinted with permission from the publisher.

Rainier Bars (page 115) contributed by Glenna Blackett.
Seeds of Change is a registered trademark of Seeds of Change, Inc. in Santa Fe.

When the sunflowers on pages 24–63 are grown under different conditions (including differences in soil, climate, and space between plants) than they were for this book, the results may vary. Color will vary only slightly; height and head size may vary more.

Library of Congress Cataloging-in-Publication Data:
Flores, Barbara, 1948–
    The great sunflower book / by Barbara Flores; photography by Lois Ellen Frank
              p.   cm.
    Includes bibliographical references.
    ISBN 0-89815-837-0
    1. Sunflowers. 2. Cookery (Sunflower seeds) I. Title
SB413.S88F58   1997
635.9'3355—dc20   96-32754
                                        CIP

First printing, 1997

Printed in Hong Kong

1 2 3 4 5 – 01 00 99 98 97

For those with heavy head

who think themselves too big,

too tall, too wild, too rough,

or fading 'round the edges—

You are God's brightest flower.

Contents

ACKNOWLEDGMENTS

This book was brought into bloom by an extraordinary seed company: Seeds of Change, Inc. in Santa Fe, New Mexico. Thank you to their Vice President and Director of Agriculture, Howard-Yana Shapiro, Ph.D., for committing the company's resources to my project and offering inspiration and direction—especially regarding sunflowers' rich Native American roots. Most of the sunflowers shown in this book were grown in Seeds of Change's research plots in the Willamette Valley of central Oregon and the Rio Grande Valley of northern New Mexico under the direction of Seeds of Change's Director of Research, Alan Kapuler, Ph.D. Some of the rare and beautiful sunflowers, such as tiger's eye and dragon's fire, have been patiently and ingeniously developed by Alan Kapuler. Alan and Howard generously shared their expertise by writing the text in the identification section. In the spirit of the Native Americans, the first developers of sunflowers, Seeds of Change holds to the philosophy that their seed and their knowledge is to be shared. It belongs to all of us on the planet.

The intricately detailed photographs come from Lois Ellen Frank, also of Santa Fe. Her camera lens has a magical way of capturing the grace and vulnerability of sunflowers. And I thank Jonathan Chester, Stan Herd, Kusra Kapuler, and Scott Vlaun for contributing their remarkable photographs. Kusra has documented the work of her father, Alan Kapuler, and shares his joy of orchids and other plants. Thanks also to Donald Smith, one of the country's first and most knowledgable sunflower agronomists, for answering questions and confirming additional variety names.

Other sunflower contributors were Ginger McMahan, for her Hopi dye sunflower, and Sigco Products Inc. of Breckinridge, Minnesota, for donating commercial food varieties. The folks at the National Sunflower Association in Bismark, North Dakota, were invaluable—they provided information, photographs, and many recipes.

I'm indebted to my husband and three teenagers for eating many weeks worth of sunflower recipes. I'm especially grateful to my youngest child, Maggie, our recipe tester, who was the original natural-food addict of the family. From the time she could walk, she ate out of the back garden…lemons, plums, apples…and could always be recognized by the berry stains on her T-shirt. She reminds me of Buffalo Bird Woman, the Hidatsa farmer who said, "We spent our days in the garden; we ate when we were hungry."

Thank you to the people at Ten Speed Press—especially Phil Wood, Kirsty Melville, and Donna Latte. I'm also indebted to David Hinds and his direction on the sunflower poster, which was the precursor to this book. He's more than an employer; he's a friend and mentor who listens, advises, clears the path, greases the wheels, then puts me in the driver's seat and hands me the reins. Creating *The Great Sunflower Book* has been a wonderful ride.

Visiting with Howard-Yana Shapiro during the research phase of this project brought me in touch with a book entitled *Buffalo Bird Woman's Garden* from the Minnesota Historical Society Press. Buffalo Bird Woman was a Hidatsa Native American farmer born in 1839 who cultivated corn, squash, beans, and sunflowers on the rich lowland banks of the Missouri River. The detailed information she offered about her life and garden was meticulously transcribed by anthropologist Gilbert L. Wilson. A portion of her book is devoted entirely to sunflowers, which was a joyous discovery for me because my search for information on the cultivation of sunflowers prior to 1900 was like looking for a needle in a haystack. Though today sunflowers are very profitable for oil and seed businesses, many early farmers treated the sunflower as a weed and focused on more easily hulled crops such as wheat and rye. Twenty-five years ago, the state of Iowa even drafted a bill declaring the sunflower a noxious weed.

> *One man gathers what another man spills.*
> —ROBERT HUNTER

Buffalo Bird Woman felt differently. She describes her gardens of corn and beans ringed in sunflowers, and the days of the young girls who sat as garden-watchers to keep out gophers, crows, or mischievous young boys. She and her garden-watchers sang to their plants: "We cared for our crops in those days as we would care for a child, for we Indian people loved our garden just as a mother loves her children...."

Her words touched on my own memories of growing up on the banks of the Menominee River in Wisconsin among corn and sunflowers. The Native American's gardening traditions were gone then, but the riverbank was rich with green woods, wildflowers, blossoms, birds, and rabbits. There were fields of tall corn, and roadsides sprouting wild sunflowers and tiger lilies. As a child, I wandered through the sunflowers singing made-up songs because I liked being where everything was bigger than I was. Sunflowers were easy to talk to because they looked at you and came in families.

At that time, I never associated the sunflowers that grew near the Menominee River with the Menominee Native Americans. The land had lost its history. But I learned later that the native peoples in this country were the first to appreciate and cultivate this flower. By picking seeds from the biggest heads to plant, they selected the giant sunflowers we know today. For three thousand years, they selected this plant for its seed and tended the crops with bone hoes and antler rakes. And with respect, love, ceremony, and song they grew the first towering, single-headed plants we know as the sunflower.

Author Barbara Flores under a Russian mammoth that sprang up from discarded birdseed

HISTORY

of an American Weed

Weeds in one place can become treasures in another, and this has been the case with the sunflower. Native to North America, there are approximately fifty species, most of which are native to the United States.

The first people to cultivate the sunflower were the Native Americans—archaeological evidence such as carbon-14 dating indicates that its seeds were a valued food item for roughly three thousand years in New Mexico, Arizona, and the Missouri/Mississippi Basin. Wild species of sunflowers were selected for large seed heads, and among some tribes, equal care was given to these plants as that which was given to the primary staples of corn, squash, and beans. Some of the harvested seeds were parched and pounded between smooth stones until they were the consistency of meal, which was then used in soups, drinks, or combined with the bone marrow of buffalo or deer and baked into cakes. Or, the seeds were boiled to separate the oil, which was skimmed off the top of the water and put to a variety of culinary and cosmetic (hair oil) uses. Even the seed hulls were used: the blue-black hulls of some species (most notably the Hopi dye, page 30) were used to obtain a purple dye that decorated baskets, textiles, and bodies. Finally, the roots of sunflowers were often used as medi-

> *What is a weed? For me a weed is a plant out of place.*
>
> —DONALD CULCROSS PEATTIE

Harvesting sunflowers in North Dakota, circa 1920. Reprinted with permission from NDSU Archives, Fargo.

cine for, among other things, snakebites and rheumatism.

Most of the sunflowers in the Native Americans' gardens were the large, single-headed variety. Clearly, the tall sunflowers that we most frequently see today have been intentionally selected for their large heads for many hundreds of years. Yet this appreciation of sunflowers was not shared by farmers of European descent until fairly recently—most preferred the easier-to-hull wheat, rye, and corn. In fact, most gardening textbooks from the nineteenth century did not even mention sunflower seed as a source of food. And until 1976, when Dr. Charles Heiser wrote *Sunflowers*, there were almost no books devoted to the subject. Obviously, sunflowers have made a resounding comeback!

Though they did not really become a major United States crop until the 1970s, sunflower seeds were certainly appreciated early on by the Europeans, who were introduced to them

upon Columbus' return from his voyages. In 1568, the Belgian herbalist Dodonaeus wrote a

description of this "new" single-headed plant, complete with a woodcut illustration. During this period, sunflowers were grown in gardens throughout western Europe. Czar Peter I of Russia (Peter the Great) traveled to the Netherlands in 1697 and encountered sunflowers for the first time. He enthusiasti-

1568 woodcut by Dodonaeus

cally carried fertile seed samples back to Russia, where, initially, only horticulturists at the St. Petersburg Botanical Garden grew them. But soon, farmers in central Russia, blessed with thick black soil, were producing larger and healthier plants than western Europeans had ever seen—some grew to fifteen feet. Sunflower seed rapidly became *the* source of oil for Russians, who led (and continue to lead) the way in the development of sunflowers as a major world food source. The plants were too

WORLD'S RECORD

The largest sunflower head ever measured was thirty-two and a half inches in diameter. It was grown in Canada. At the other end of the measuring stick, the shortest sunflower was just over two inches. It was grown in Oregon using a bonsai technique. And the tallest sunflower plant on record stretched twenty-five feet, five inches. It was grown in the Netherlands.

—Guinness Book of World Records

The winner of this 1990 sunflower contest in Redwood City, California, measures twenty-three inches in diameter.

new to have been proscribed by the Russian Orthodox Church, and were thus not included in a list of high-fat crops that could not be eaten during Lent. Followers of the Church could obey the law to the letter and still obtain a much-needed high-energy food source by eating sunflower kernels. Another virtue of sunflower seeds soon became clear to the rural people of eastern Europe—sunflower oil has a lower setting point than animal fats, which means it remains liquid at lower temperatures and can thus be poured during very cold weather. To this day, sunflower seeds are a primary snack food in Russia.

It took immigrants from Russia—by way of Canada—to reintroduce the sunflower seed as a noteworthy food source for modern-day Americans. The immigrants were Mennonites who

Presidential candidate Alfred Landon, known as the "Kansas sunflower," used a sunflower motif for his 1936 campaign button.

settled on the Canadian prairies during the 1870s. While in Russia the Mennonites had grown their own sunflowers, and upon leaving their home took with them seeds of the Russian mammoth. By the 1880s, Russian mammoth seeds were being offered for sale in the catalogs of some U.S. seed companies. It was around this time that a Russian agronomist developed a sunflower with almost twice as much oil as standard varieties, and its reputation spread across the country soon after the seeds made their first appearance. Sunflowers are now the second-most-important world oil crop, after soybeans. The North American sunflower, the Native American staple that was a weed to American farmers but found favor and acclaim in foreign lands, finally returned home with much celebration and fanfare.

SUNFLOWER LEGEND

It is said that when the Mormons left Missouri in the 1830s in search of a place where they could worship freely, the first wagon train scattered a trail of sunflower seeds to mark their trail—when the next wagon train set out the following summer, the people were easily guided to their new home in Utah by the path of sunflowers that stretched out before them.

Owl Woman, a Native American who lived at the turn of the century, gathers sunflowers in this photograph from 1914.

BUFFALO BIRD WOMAN'S GARDEN

The following is excerpted from *Buffalo Bird Woman's Garden: Agriculture of the Hidatsa Indians*, as told to Gilbert L. Wilson, reprint edition, St. Paul: Minnesota Historical Society Press, 1987.

Buffalo Bird Woman, known in Hidatsa as Maxidiwiac, was born about 1839 in an earth lodge along the Knife River in present-day North Dakota. In 1845 her people moved upstream and built Like-a-fishhook Village, which they shared with the Mandan and Arikara. There Buffalo Bird Woman grew up to become an expert gardener of the Hidatsa tribe. Using agricultural practices centuries old, she and the women of her family grew corn, beans, squash, and sunflowers in the fertile bottomlands of the Missouri River....

It was our Indian rule to keep our fields very sacred. We did not like to quarrel about our garden lands:…if one were selfish and quarrelsome, and tried to seize land belonging to another, we thought some evil would come upon him, as that some one of his family should die.…

The first seed that we planted in the spring was sunflower seed. Ice breaks on the Missouri about the first week in April; and we planted sunflower seed as soon after as the soil could be worked. Our native name for the lunar month that corresponds most nearly to April, is Mapi'-o'ce-mi'di, or Sunflower-planting-moon.…

Usually we planted sunflowers only around the edges of a field. The hills were placed eight or nine paces apart; for we never sowed sunflowers thickly. We thought a field surrounded thus by a sparse-sown row of sunflowers, had a handsome appearance.…

The sunflower heads were dried face downward, that the sun falling on the back of the head might dry and shrink the fiber, thus loosening the seeds. The heads were laid flat on the bare roof, without skins or other protection beneath. If a storm threatened, the unthreshed heads were gathered up and borne into

SUNFLOWERS AS MEDICINE

Some Native American peoples applied juice from the sunflower's stem as a remedy for cuts and bruises. The roots were boiled, and the warm liquid was used as a liniment. This was also used to alleviate the inflammation and discomfort of poison oak, poison ivy, snakebites, and rheumatism. In Russia, a popular remedy for rheumatism was to combine cut-up sunflower heads, soap chips, and vodka that was left in the sun for nine days. This potent mixture was then rubbed on the body. Elsewhere throughout the world, teas made from the stems of oil-rich sunflower plants was drunk to cure coughs and fevers.

the lodge; but they were left on the roof overnight, if the weather was fair....

To thresh the heads, a skin was spread and the heads laid on it face downward, and beaten with a stick.... The large heads, left on the roof over night, were sometimes caught by the frost; and meal made from their seed was more oily than that from unfrosted seed. Sometimes we took the threshed seed out of doors and let it get frosted, so as to bring out this oiliness. Frosting the seeds did not kill them....

To make sunflower meal the seeds were first roasted, or parched. This was done in a clay pot.... I threw into the pot two or three double-handfuls of the seeds and as they parched, I stirred them with a little stick, to keep them from burning.

Now and then I took out a seed and bit it; if the kernel was soft and gummy, I knew the parching was not done; but when it bit dry and crisp, I knew the seeds were cooked and I dipped them out with a horn spoon into a wooden bowl.... Parching the seeds caused them to crack open somewhat. The parched seeds were pounded in the corn mortar to make meal....

Sunflower meal of the parched seeds was also used to make sunflower seed balls; these were important articles of diet in olden times, and had a particular use.... When worn with fatigue or overcome with sleep and weariness, the warrior took out his sunflower-seed ball, and nibbled at it to refresh himself. It was amazing what effect nibbling at the sunflower-seed ball had. If the warrior was weary, he began to feel fresh again; if sleepy, he grew wakeful. Sometimes the warrior kept his sunflower-seed ball in his flint case that hung always at his belt over his right hip. It was quite a general custom in my tribe for a warrior or hunter to carry one of these sunflower-seed balls....

In a story that Buffalo Bird Woman once related, she described a "watching stage" that was built under a tree in a garden by a river. The stage was a platform made of wood from which two girls watched the garden and sang "watch-garden songs." She said that the girls did this to

> *It's not enough to talk to plants; you also have to listen.*
>
> — DAVID BERGMAN

"make the garden grow, just as people sing to a baby to make it be quiet and feel good."

Buffalo Bird Woman was saddened to see that the traditional ways of her people were being lost to the younger generation. At the end of the book's Introduction she is quoted as follows:

I am an old woman now. The buffaloes and black-tail deer are gone.... We no longer live in an earth lodge, but in a house with chimneys; and my son's wife cooks by a stove. But for me, I cannot forget our old ways.

SUNFLOWERS IN CEREMONY

Hopi peoples wore sunflowers in their hair during some of their ceremonies, and drew the plant on the walls of their kivas, or sacred lodges. The Lakota's sun dance ceremony, which was officially banned by missionaries for over fifty years, also featured sunflowers—they were depicted on medallions that the dancers wore on their chests. The medallions were an important symbol of strength and endurance because the dancers were required to dance non-stop for days!

VINCENT VAN GOGH, SUNFLOWER ENTHUSIAST

Van Gogh had a love affair
with sunflowers: during the
last three years of his short life
he began painting sunflowers
in France and eventually created more than fifteen paintings featuring the plants.
Cézanne didn't do a single
one, nor did Picasso. In one of
his most famous paintings, a
vase with fourteen sunflowers,
there are both single- and
double-petalled types— fore-
seeing the popularity of lion's
mane, teddy bear, and supermane (pages 44–45). Van
Gogh has even been credited
with starting the current sunflower craze—sunflower
bouquets became wildly popular after the much publicized
exhibit of his later paintings
at the Metropolitan Museum
of Art in 1987.

Sunflowers, 1888, by Gogh, Vincent van (1853-90)
Neue Pinakothek, Munich/Giraudon/Bridgeman Art
Library, Londo

THE
SUNFLOWERS

*S*unflowers are daisies, members of the Aster family, which together with the orchids are the two largest families of plants on earth. The primary distinguishing feature of the daisy family is the grouping of many tiny flowers, called florets, into a head that is surrounded by ray petals. Interestingly, the flower tops of dill, parsnips, carrots, and caraway have clusters of tiny flowers that are also very similar. Biochemically, they and the sunflowers have certain genetic material in common. In short, the sunflower is more closely related to the carrot or dill than it is to a rose or lily.

Helianthus, the sunflowers' genus, contains about fifty species, including both wild and cultivated varieties. Twenty belong to the species *Helianthus annuus*, of which all varieties are annuals, meaning they only grow for a single season. But thirty species are perennials, living for several years. Probably the most widely cultivated of the perennials is the food plant *H. tuberosus*, also known as Jerusalem artichoke, sunchoke, or sunroot. Several varieties of this species are grown, most popular of which is the French mammoth, with its white-skinned, knobby tubers. Another widely grown perennial is the ornamental *H. maximiliani* (page 60).

Of the annual species, undoubtedly the most popular in cultivation is *H. annuus*, which has been crossed to almost all of the other annual species. One cross (*H. annuus* to *H. petiolaris*) resulted in flowers without pollen. This generation of male sterile lines has been used to improve the oil content, pest resistance, and productivity of commercial oil seed sunflowers.

The sunflowers' wild progenitor is most common in the Midwest, Southwest, and West, but today's numerous varieties flourish coast to coast—from the wet, mucky soils of Florida, to the Mojave Desert, to the woodlands of the Pacific Northwest. Population sizes vary widely. One variety that used to thrive in the pre–Los Angeles swamps of southern California has not been found for several years and is likely extinct. At least three more species are in danger of joining it: *H. exilis*, *H. paradoxus*, and *H. multiflorus*.

A few American Indian groups (such as the Hopi and Havasupais in Arizona and the Mandans and Arikaras in North Dakota) still grow the same varieties of sunflowers that their ancestors did. These varieties are also on the verge of extinction, although efforts are being made to save them not only for their historical value but for their valuable germ plasm, which may help develop new sunflowers for future generations.

Although it is easy to think of the sunflower as a single flower, it is actually a composite of small florets, which, arranged in circles, comprise the face of the sunflower head. Each floret has its own ovary, stigma, style, and anthers, and produces a single seed. A large sunflower head, perhaps a foot across, can have as many as eight thousand florets. The outer ring of florets has large ray petals, which can be a greenish yellow when young, turning a darker yellow orange on maturity. In double sunflowers, the inner florets have elongated and quilled petals that give them the appearance of a fluffy chrysanthemum.

All sunflower seeds are edible, but the seeds of the small ornamentals are too small to be of use commercially. Those grown just for the seeds—confectionery sunflowers—of course have larger seeds, are generally related to the Russian mammoth and Israeli types, and sport the familiar black-and-white or gray-striped hulls. The oil seed varieties have smaller, thinner hulls that have been hybridized and selected to have a much higher oil content with less protein. Most of the commercial varieties, both ornamentals and those used for food, are hybrids.

THE CHERNOBYL SUNFLOWER CLEAN-UP PROJECT

In 1994, researchers in the Ukraine began using sunflowers to help clean a highly contaminated pond near Chernobyl. Yes, sunflowers. They are planted on floating gardens—ordinary rafts with a small pit for soil—with their roots allowed to dangle into the water. The roots absorb dangerous radionuclides, and after about three weeks the plants are disposed of as radioactive waste. Remarkably, just fifty to sixty sunflowers are able to clean up a seventy-five-square-meter pond.

bracts
(green outer
leaves)

florets

ray petals

*Single-stalked
Tarahumara sunflower*

RUSSIAN MAMMOTH

DERIVED FROM *HELIANTHUS ANNUUS*

Perhaps the best known of the sunflowers for its huge, thick stalk and giant single flower. It is one of the fastest growing plants of the annual garden. The diameter of the head can be fourteen inches or more, and the stalk can reach beyond twelve feet. Seeds have large, thick shells striped black or gray, and the flowers have a ring of orange-yellow ray petals with small, brown, cuplike florets that cover the

center. This is an heirloom confectionery sunflower grown for its kernels; also widely used in harvest arrangements. About a third of the kernel is oil, and about a fifth is protein. A large head holds more than a thousand seeds, but heads with more than five thousand are not that uncommon. *(Similar varieties may also be known as Paul Bunyan, mammoth grey stripe, giant, and Russian giant.)*

GLORIOSA

DERIVED FROM *HELIANTHUS ANNUUS*

Selected from a mixture of small-seeded polyheaded sunflowers, this variety is distinguished by the reddish to purple-brown spot on each of the yellow-orange ray petals. This gives an attractive reddish ring on each flower, similar in appearance to the gloriosa daisy (*Rudbeckia hirta*) from which it derives its name. This sunflower grows up to eight feet, with up to thirty branches carrying six-inch flowers. (*Similar varieties may also be known as autumn beauty and sunset.*)

LION'S MANE

DERIVED FROM *HELIANTHUS ANNUUS*

The double sunflower of Vincent van Gogh's paintings. This beautiful, multibranched, polyheaded cultivar holds ten to fifteen yellow-orange flowers that are six inches across. Plants grow six to eight feet tall. A recently popular dwarf variety growing four to six feet tall is called sungold. An even smaller variety is called teddy bear. Note: In the generations that have been developed from crossing lion's mane with gloriosa, there are some lion's manes with long outer ray petals. (*Similar varieties may also be known as chrysanthemum, orange sun, and giant sungold.*)

CONFECTION

DERIVED FROM
HELIANTHUS ANNUUS

*T*he confection sunflower is the United States' commercial hybrid of the Russian mammoth; it is grown primarily for seed production. In late summer, its large, twelve-inch heads create a sea of yellow across fields all over the Midwest. Like the Russian mammoth, confection seeds are gray with white stripes and possess a meaty inner kernel.

HOPI DYE

DERIVED FROM *HELIANTHUS ANNUUS*

A traditional American Indian sunflower with yellow-orange ray petals, 6-inch flowers, and a dark center. The purplish black shells of the seeds were used by Native Americans to make red or indigo dyes.

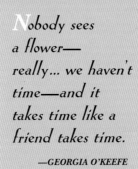

*Nobody sees
a flower—
really... we haven't
time—and it
takes time like a
friend takes time.*

—GEORGIA O'KEEFE

WILD SUNFLOWER

DERIVED FROM *HELIANTHUS ANNUUS*

This hardy native wildflower grows three to ten feet high and is found in fields and along roadsides across most of the United States. It is the ancestor of the giant cultivated sunflower and has been useful in commercial breeding because it is a good source of disease-resistant genes. *(A similar variety may also be known as common sunflower.)*

SUNBEAM

DERIVED FROM *HELIANTHUS ANNUUS*

Popular florist ornamental with yellow-orange petals. There's no messy pollen, as this is a male sterile variety. The four-inch flowers are long lasting, with green centers that darken as the flowers mature. The strong, tall (up to five feet) stems and absence of pollen make it a choice variety for bouquets and arrangements. These grow well in cool greenhouses during the short days of winter. Two similar pollenless varieties with lemon-yellow flowers are the sunrich lemon and sunrich orange, developed in Japan.

LEMON

DERIVED FROM *HELIANTHUS ANNUUS*

A strikingly beautiful flower with bright, lemon-yellow petals and a dark brown central eye. Derived from the gloriosa (page 26). This poly-headed variety grows up to eight feet and possesses six-inch flowers. During a three-year development project with the gloriosa, in which five thousand plants were cultivated, only three grand lemons, with these lovely flowers, were produced. *(Similar varieties may be known as lemon queen, sunrise, and valentine.)*

TARAHUMARA WHITE SHELLED

DERIVED FROM *HELIANTHUS ANNUUS*

A single stalk with a large, single head is produced by this traditional Tarahumara Native American variety. Plants grow seven to eight feet tall, and the all-yellow flower is ten to twelve inches across. It is moderately thin shelled and is grown primarily for its edible kernels. The seeds have distinctive, pure-white hulls.

FOR THE BIGGEST BLOOMS...

Experts at the National Sunflower Association in North Dakota point out that best way to get the biggest blooms is to give your seeds plenty of room to grow. For example, although Russian mammoths have the biggest heads, they won't reach their full potential if their seeds are planted too close together. However, if you plant the seeds with lots of extra room inbetween, your sunflowers will thank you by growing the biggest heads they possibly can.

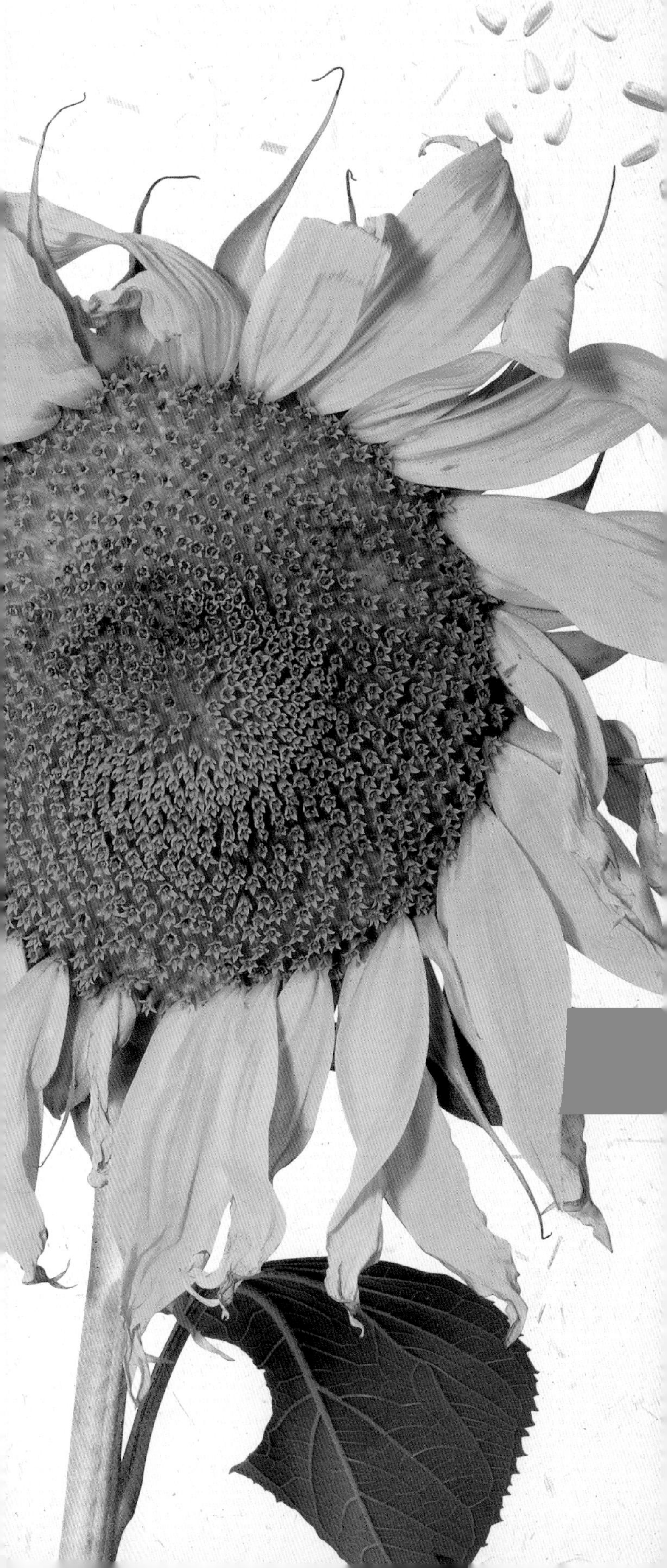

TAWNY LEMON

DERIVED FROM *HELIANTHUS ANNUUS*

This plant is derived from the polyheaded gloriosa (page 26). Plants grow up to eight feet, and the six-inch flowers are unique in coloration: the petals are yellow with an overlay of reddish brown that gives a tawny, amber appearance, in contrast to the dark, central eye. A "grow out" of several hundred gloriosa plants produced around six with this unusual sunset color.

AMBER

DERIVED FROM *HELIANTHUS ANNUUS*

Mixes of yellow, red, and bronze sunflowers will produce some amber varieties such as this, which will grow to six feet and have four-to six-inch flowers. *(Similar varieties may also be known as chianti, red prado, autumn gold, or Inca jewels.)*

EVENING SUN

DERIVED FROM *HELIANTHUS ANNUUS*

A very rare color variety. The dark, red flowers are four to six inches, and the plants grow to six feet with ten to fifteen branches. The seeds are quite small and greatly relished by birds. *(A similar variety may also be known as prado red.)*

SILVERLEAF

DERIVED FROM
HELIANTHUS ARGOPHYLLUS

Fuzzy, silvery leaves make this plant especially beautiful. The daisylike flowers are yellow orange with brown centers and grow to about four inches across. Plants grow up to five feet tall and have rather small seeds, which are very attractive to finches. These flower two weeks to a month later than the *Helianthus annuus* varieties.

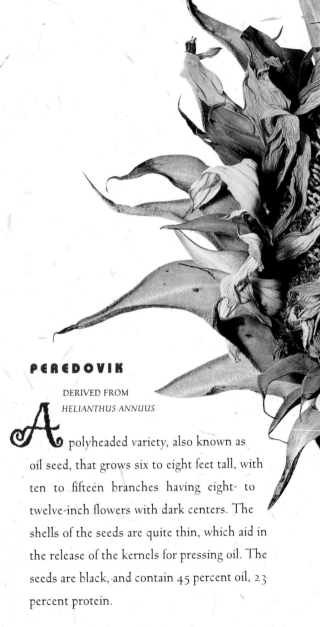

PEREDOVIK

DERIVED FROM
HELIANTHUS ANNUUS

A polyheaded variety, also known as oil seed, that grows six to eight feet tall, with ten to fifteen branches having eight- to twelve-inch flowers with dark centers. The shells of the seeds are quite thin, which aid in the release of the kernels for pressing oil. The seeds are black, and contain 45 percent oil, 23 percent protein.

SUNBRIGHT

DERIVED FROM *HELIANTHUS ANNUUS*

This cheery ornamental with its long three- to four-foot stem and seven-inch flowers has become very popular with florists because it is ideal in many ways for decorating the home: it is pollenless; the flowers are long lasting and sturdy, and the plant is available all year because it grows well in greenhouses. Its dark blue to black centers provide an attractive contrast with its bright yellow ray petals. An orange-petaled variety (opposite page, bottom) is sold as **endurance orange**. *(Varieties similar to endurance orange may also be known as tangina and sonja.)*

THOSE RESOURCEFUL PIONEERS...

Some American pioneers figured out how to make fabric from the coarse fiber of sunflower stalks. Another use of dry stalks was kindling. The Canadian pioneers took this one step further—they made logs out of compressed seed hulls!

SUPERMANE

DERIVED FROM
HELIANTHUS ANNUUS

Possesses the thickest petal mane yet discovered. Plants grow up to six feet, depending on their planting density —growth is stunted if they are too close together. But if grown three to five feet apart, they are like small Christmas trees, having a pyramidal shape and thirty to fifty branches. The flowers are about six inches across, fully double, well spread out, and soft to the touch.

DRAGON'S FIRE

DERIVED FROM *HELIANTHUS ANNUUS*

One of the rarest sunflowers of all—it only arises from the infrequent self-pollination of tiger's eye (page below). This stunning, dahlia-like flower is found roughly once in two thousand crossings. The six-inch flowers are fully double, with a mosaic of color in the center—red, amber, and yellow-orange petalets surrounded by larger yellow-orange ray petals. The plants are polyheaded, up to six feet tall, and possess ten to fifteen branches.

Dragon's fire and tiger's eye are created from the cross-pollination of the red-ringed gloriosa (left) and lion's mane (right).

TIGER'S EYE

DERIVED FROM *HELIANTHUS ANNUUS*

Cross-pollination of a red-ringed gloriosa and a lion's mane (page 48) gave rise to this remarkable-looking hybrid. Subsequent generations have stabilized the cross. The large, partly double, central eye is a mosaic of colors—red, brown, purple, and yellow-orange. Plants are polyheaded, with fifteen to twenty branches and six-inch flowers.

TIGER'S EYE VARIATIONS

(Parent flowers are shown opposite, at bottom.)

Red-ringed gloriosa   Lion's mane

ISRAELI SINGLE HEAD

DERIVED FROM *HELIANTHUS ANNUUS*

Derived from the Russian mammoth (page 24), this is a large, single-headed plant with flowers that are ten to fourteen inches and sturdy stalks that are five to six feet tall. The seed shells are thick, with black-and-white stripes.

> "Just living is
> not enough,"
> said the butterfly,
> "one must have
> sunshine,
> freedom, and
> a little flower."
> —HANS CHRISTIAN ANDERSEN

DWARF SUNSPOT

DERIVED FROM *HELIANTHUS ANNUUS*

This recently developed plant offers full-sized, ten-inch flowers on dwarf plants just one to two feet tall. It can be planted in a pot as small as eight inches. Despite its abbreviated height, it still produces a load of seeds that are tasty when roasted and also perfect for birdseed. This is a favorite with children. *(One similar variety may be known as big smile.)*

SUNSHINE

DERIVED FROM *HELIANTHUS ANNUUS*

A fairly new hybrid, having yellow-orange flowers with a large, central, golden eye. This is a six- to eight-foot variety, with ten to fifteen branches per plant. Flowers are six inches across.

ORANGE KING

DERIVED FROM *HELIANTHUS ANNUUS*

Related to the sunshine (above) and similar varieties that have large, golden, central eyes. The color is a mixture of yellow, gold, and orange. When a gold double crosses with a yellow-orange single, a golden tiger's eye arises. When this crosses with itself or with a yellow-orange double, the orange king arises. These plants are six feet tall, multibranched, and polyflorous with six-inch flowers.

LEMONADE

DERIVED FROM *HELIANTHUS ANNUUS*

These are lovely, unusual dwarf plants. The lemon-yellow, double flowers are only four inches across, and the plants are only three feet tall. They have the large double eye of a lion's mane (page 26) with the large outer petals of the more common varieties.

LEMON TIGER'S EYE

DERIVED FROM *HELIANTHUS ANNUUS*

When grand lemon (page 32) crosses with lion's mane (page 26), eventually six- to eight-inch flowers will be produced that have yellow petals with large, dark, semidouble centers as this one does.

THE SYMBOLIC SUNFLOWER

In the Victorian era, the sunflower became a symbol of American and European reaction against the repression and bleakness of the industrial age. Sunflowers were carved into the backs of chairs, glazed onto vases, wrought into iron railings, and even cast into building facades. The purity and wild spirit of the sunflower was able to symbolize a challenge to the industrial age then, and it should be no surprise that it has recently resurfaced to become a national symbol in this age of cyberspace. Now, toward the end of the twentieth century, it looks like there's no stopping this tall, golden beauty that has even been granted its own year—according to Life magazine, 1996 was the Year of the Sunflower.

MEXICAN TITHONIA

TITHONIA *ROTUNDIFOLIA*

*T*he Mexican tithonia is classified as a sunflower commercially, but genetically it is not of the genus *Helianthus*. It is a giant ornamental that grows between six and fourteen feet tall, with dozens of three-inch red and red-orange flowers that are brilliantly displayed against a thick, intensely green foliage.

ITALIAN WHITE

DERIVED FROM *HELIANTHUS ANNUUS*

*U*nusually pale, with creamy yellow petals and a dark, chocolate-colored center. Plants grow four to six feet tall with ten to twenty branches; flowers are four inches across. This variety was derived from a wild species commonly known as the cucumber leaf. The petals twist in a fashion reminiscent of the cactus-flowered dahlias and some of the spider chrysanthemums. Recently, Italian whites have become very popular. The lovely flowers and stems are somewhat frail, however, and are better left in the garden than placed in bouquets. *(One similar variety may be known as vanilla ice.)*

Earth laughs in flowers.

—RALPH WALDO EMERSON

MAXIMILIAN

DERIVED FROM
HELIANTHUS MAXIMILIANII

Unlike the vast majority of sunflowers, this variety is a perennial. It is a hardy, sturdy plant, probably the most widely grown perennial because it is so useful along hedge rows, fences, and watercourses. The stalks grow between six and eight feet tall and possess multiflowered clusters of yellow-orange flowers two to three inches across that are particularly favored by birds. Easy propagation is by division of the root clumps, either in the fall or early spring. *(In the wild, this is known as the prairie sunflower.)*

JERUSALEM ARTICHOKE

DERIVED FROM *HELIANTHUS TUBEROSUS*

(also known as sunroot or sunchoke)

Unlike the vast majority of sunflowers, this variety is a perennial. Its clusters of yellow-orange flowers are three inches across, and its stalks are six to eight feet tall. After a full growing season, masses of edible tubers can be harvested from below the soil surface. The shape, flavor, and color depend on the particular variety of artichoke grown—most common is the French white mammoth, with knobby tubers. The fuseau variety has elongated, pale yellow tubers, and the magenta variety has tubers with white flesh and intensely purple-colored skin.

Comparing the flowers of Helianthus annuus *(right)* with those of Helianthus tuberosus *(left)*.

GARDENING
TIPS

*S*unflowers are remarkably easy to garden—in fact, they often self-seed, leaving you nothing to do. But should you choose to take a more proactive role, cross-fertilization can give rise to some stunning new plants. Following is a fairly simple technique for breeding your own sunflowers.

First, choose two varieties that you find attractive and distinctive. The more different they are from each other, the more fun it will be to cross them. Be sure to plant them at the same time, so that they will flower at roughly the same time. Also, note that sunflowers mature their stigmas and pollen radially from the outside of the flower to the inside, so you'll only be able to pollinate a few florets on a given flower on a given day.

A sunflower's lighter outer ring in the center disc is caused by opened florets, which are releasing pollen.

BREED YOUR OWN SUNFLOWERS

1. With a magnifying glass, watch for the pollen to mature—this will happen first on the outer ring of florets. (Tease apart the central petalets to find the pollen.)

2. With tweezers, place the pollen on a few dozen of the stigmas of the other plant. Make a mark on the back of the flower head with a water insoluble pen to show where the crossing was done.

3. Place a paper bag over the head to keep out any other pollen, which may be carried by insects or wind.

4. When the head matures, carefully collect the seeds all around the area you pollinated.

5. Dry these in a food dehydrator at 95° for four hours.

6. Store the dried seeds in a glass jar, away from light and at room temperature, until the next planting season.

7. The following season, plant your seed in pots. When the plants are a foot tall, replant them in the garden.

8. Any two sunflower varieties can be cross bred as long as they produce pollen. You can even cross the very large-headed flowers with smaller varieties, but not with any predictability.

Here are a few suggested crosses:

gloriosa x lion's mane

gloriosa x lemon

evening sun x lion's mane

evening sun x sunshine

gloriosa x supermane

lion's mane x evening sun

lemon x lion's mane

The parent flowers in the center are lion's mane (on left) and gloriosa (on right); offspring of the two are in the outside ring and include tiger's eye, dragon's fire, and sunshine.

In the spring, once the danger of frost has passed, plant seeds in a spot that receives full sun. Or, seeds can be given a head start by planting them first in a greenhouse—upon germination they can be transferred outside. These indoor-sprouted seedlings can bloom two weeks to a month before the traditionally seeded ones flower. Generally, if seeds are planted in the greenhouse in February or March, the plants flower sixty-five to seventy-five days later. Some varieties, however, bloom as early as fifty-five days after planting. In the temperate regions of the Pacific Northwest, many begin to flower in June and stick around until late November. But such a long season cannot be counted on in harsher climates. A useful trick for extending the blooming period is to stagger your plantings about a week apart.

Sunflowers are not particularly fussy about soil, but they do appreciate it well drained and loose. Plant the seeds an inch deep and about two feet apart. If you plan to provide a stake for your plants, insert it now—sticking it in after the plants have started growing may injure their roots. In dry climates, water thoroughly at least once a week. (Most sunflowers are considered to be drought resistant, but regular watering will give them maximum height.) Most importantly, they need full sun—the hotter, the better. A three- to four-inch mulch will help conserve moisture and thwart weeds.

TO SPROUT SEEDS IN SOIL

Punch a few draining holes in a large foil pan (approximately 9 by 13 inches). Place a one-inch layer of potting soil inside. Soak a half cup of raw, unhulled seeds overnight. Avoid using chemically treated seeds in garden seed packages. After they've been drained, scatter the seeds over the soil and cover with another quarter-inch layer of soil. Place a blanket

of dampened newspaper over the top of the pan
and a cookie sheet underneath (to catch excess
water). Keep the soil moist until sprouts germi-
nate. Remove the newspaper from germinating
sprouts and give them light from a sunny window or a warm porch. Harvest in ten to fourteen
days, when the first two leaves unfurl and
turn green. These soil-grown shoots
will be taller than the jar-grown ones
(see page 72).

A CHILD'S LESSON

What better way is there to teach a child about nature
than by planting sunflowers together? Little fingers can
poke a hole in the earth, place a seed, and cover it up
again. Impatient youngsters will not have to wait long for
results—in just ten days little sprouts will be popping up,
some wearing their striped seed shell for a hat. Growing
high and fast, their Jack-and-the-Beanstalk growth is a
feast of fantasy. Children will watch for the first appearance of harvestable seeds, will have great fun removing the
seeds from the head, and will delight in bringing to the
kitchen table something they had a hand in cultivating. In
winter, they can be shown how to offer the fruits of their
labor to hungry birds and squirrels.

JAR-GROWN SPROUTS

*S*prouting is easy, and the vitamin-rich results can be used in sandwiches or salads just as you would use alfalfa or bean sprouts. Start with a half cup of raw, unhulled seed (again, use fresh, not packaged seed). Soak overnight to soften the seed case, then drain and place them in a glass jar covered with an air-permeable cloth. Place this in a moderately cool (70°) cabinet, away from bright light. The seed will dry out if there is too much warmth and light, and will mold if the temperature is too cold. After sprouts appear, begin rinsing them every morning and evening, tilting the jar slightly to drain excess

water. In several days to a week, you will find delicate green sprouts about two or three inches long. To retain their freshness, store these in the refrigerator in plastic bags lined with paper towels.

These ornamental sunflowers were colored bright
orange by placing the stems in water with red dye.

TIPS ON SHELLING SEEDS

To shell seeds in quantity, first break them up with a rolling pin, hammer, or a short spin in the blender. Then put the mixture in a water-filled container, and stir vigorously. The meaty kernels will sink to the bottom and the shells will float. Don't worry—when they're dry, these kernels will roast nicely.

DRYING SUNFLOWERS

Dried seed heads make attractive harvest arrangements, and smaller ornamentals look beautiful in wreaths or bouquets. Pick the plants just before the flowers have reached their peak. Make sure they are dry, and hang them upside down in a dimly lit, ventilated area such as a pantry or outdoor storage shed. This will retain their color. But if you're not too concerned about maintaining their color, dry them in a window, where everyone can enjoy them. That's what I do, simply because I find them much too beautiful to hide in a dimly lit area!

COOKING

with Sunflower Seeds

*T*hank goodness *real* food is coming back as an alternative to packaged food with its dyes, chemicals, and preservatives. Think about it— there is live genetic material in the unhulled sunflower seed that is capable of producing a glorious, ten-foot plant! No wonder the seeds are a high-energy food source.

Unhulled kernels have a twelve-month shelf life, but hulled, toasted kernels will only last a few months and should be kept in the refrigerator. Note that raw kernels will turn green during baking unless the recipe has acidic ingredients such as lemon juice, vinegar, or fruit. But the green seeds are not in any way harmful and taste just as good. In fact, raw kernels are higher in nutrition than the toasted. But my preference is for toasted seeds, as they have a richer flavor. They can be tossed in by the handful in cereals, sandwiches, casseroles, salads, and just about anything else you generally enjoy snacking on. With twice as much iron as raisins, sunflower seeds make an easy-to-carry, high-energy trail mix. In general, anything with oats tastes better with sunflower seeds—especially a morning bowl of oatmeal. They also lend themselves well to any recipes with wild rice or mushrooms, especially the exotic varieties with earthy flavors such as portobellos and shiitakes. Try using sunflower seeds instead of nuts—you'll save money (especially when pine nuts are called for) and chopping time. Replace Baco-Bits™ with toasted seeds—you'll get the crunch and deep flavor without the chemicals and cholesterol. And as an added benefit, you may find yourself craving sweets less. I've discovered that eating sunflower seeds in place of sugary snacks can actually break a sugar addiction.

Sunflower seeds are 25 percent protein, making them higher in protein (surprisingly) than grains. Combining them with legumes creates a completely balanced replacement for meats and eggs. They also have a good fiber content, are rich in some B vitamins (primarily thiamin and niacin), and possess plentiful iron, calcium, and zinc. For people with high blood pressure, sunflower seeds are a good choice because they are very high in potassium but low in sodium, a balance sorely needed in the snack-food industry. Two antioxidant vitamins are found in sunflower seed oil. And of all the commonly available cooking oils, sunflower oil has the highest level of alpha-tocopherol, which is the most active form of vitamin E.

After the oil has been removed from the seeds, a high-protein cake or meal remains. While the original oil seed kernels contained 20–25 percent protein, the meal contains 60–65 percent protein. A critical aspect of this meal is its balance of amino acids—the meal is a good source of at least two of the essential amino acids, and it also contains the sulphur amino acids, which are lacking in corn. Since soybeans, the main source of seed meal in world commerce, are also lacking the sulphur acids, sunflower protein is an extremely important addition to a diet centered around corn and soybeans, as most of the world's cuisines are.

Overall, sunflower seeds are a very mineral-rich and high-energy food. Native Americans recognized this fact centuries ago—some of the warriors in the northern Midwest used ground sunflower meal and oil to form edible balls *(mapi)* that they carried in a buffalo-skin case that always hung at their belt.

Toasting Techniques

Whole seed toasting

Soak unhulled seeds in salted (or, if you choose, unsalted) water for eight hours. Drain and spread them on a large baking sheet in a single layer. Roast, stirring occasionally, at 200° for 3 hours, or until crisp.

Kernel toasting

Place a single layer of raw, hulled kernels on a shallow pan for 30–40 minutes in a 300° oven. Stir once about midway through the process. An alternative method for the less patient is to use a 325° oven for just 12 minutes, stirring once or twice during the last 5 minutes.

Quick pan toasting

Hulled seeds can also be toasted in a dry skillet on high heat for 2 to 3 minutes, stirring occasionally. Don't walk away—they'll burn very quickly.

Millet Loaf

From *Friendly Foods* by Brother Ron Pickarski.

YIELD: 8 SERVINGS

1½ cups millet
3¾ cups water
2 teaspoons sea salt
1½ cups finely diced carrots
1 cup finely diced celery
1 cup finely diced onions
1 clove garlic, minced
2 tablespoons sesame oil
1½ teaspoons dill weed
1 teaspoon dried thyme
1 cup toasted sunflower seeds
(see page 79)
3 tablespoons flour
3 tablespoons gluten flour

Rinse the millet and put it in a medium saucepan with the water and ½ teaspoon of salt. Cook the millet, covered, over medium heat for about 30 minutes or until soft; the millet should absorb all of the water.

Sauté the carrots, celery, onions, and garlic in oil for 6 minutes, or until the onions are translucent. Add the seasonings, including the remaining 1½ teaspoons of salt. Mix the cooked millet and the vegetables together, along with the sunflower seeds. Mix the two flours together and add them to the millet mixture, blending it well. Preheat oven to 400°.

Lightly oil and flour a large loaf pan. Press the millet mixture into the pan and bake for about 1 hour. (If the millet is warm when you put it in the pan, reduce the baking time to about 45 minutes.) Remove from the pan after it has cooled 10 minutes.

Opposite: Multibranched polyheaded sunflower

Petal Pasta Salad

Adapted from *Edible Flowers* by Kitty Morse.

Raw sunflower petals have a slightly bitter taste, so be sure to steam them lightly before using them.

YIELD: 3 SERVINGS

1 pound extra firm tofu, sliced into strips
½ cup bottled teriyaki marinade
8 ounces fresh pasta
1 eight-ounce bottle Italian dressing
¼ cup toasted sunflower seeds (page 79)
Petals from 2 sunflowers
6 shredded basil leaves

In a medium bowl, combine the tofu with the marinade. Let it stand, turning once or twice, for 20 to 30 minutes. Turn the oven to broil. Drain the tofu. Place it in a baking dish or on a baking sheet and broil 3 to 4 minutes on each side. Remove from the oven and let cool.

In a large pan filled with lightly salted water, cook pasta until al dente, 2 to 3 minutes. Drain well. Rinse under cold water and drain again. Transfer to a serving bowl and toss with dressing and sunflower seeds. Set aside. In a steamer set atop boiling water, steam petals for 2 minutes. Remove from heat. To assemble salad, mound pasta on a serving platter. Top artfully with steamed petals and strips of tofu. Chill for 1 hour. Sprinkle with basil before serving.

Pasta with Sunflower Kernels

Courtesy of The National Sunflower
Association.

YIELD: 4 SERVINGS

8 ounces flavored pasta (sundried
tomato or spinach)
3 sprigs parsley, chopped
3 cloves garlic, minced
1 teaspoon grated lemon peel
½ cup sunflower oil
½ teaspoon salt
½ teaspoon pepper
½ cup chopped dry-packed sundried
tomatoes
⅔ cup grated Parmesan cheese
½ cup roasted sunflower kernels (page 79)

Cook pasta and drain.

In a small skillet over medium heat, sauté
parsley, garlic, and lemon peel in the oil for just
1 minute, then remove the mixture from the
heat. Stir in the salt, pepper, and sundried
tomatoes. Transfer to a large serving bowl and
toss with the pasta, Parmesan, and sunflower
kernels until well blended.

Sunflower Dolmas

I find that making dolmas is a homey, relaxing activity best enjoyed with friends and family. Find somebody who'd like to help out, put on some Mediterranean music, and have fun.

YIELD: 35 DOLMAS

1 large onion, finely chopped
2 cloves garlic, minced
2 portobello mushrooms, or 1 pound crimini, finely chopped
¼ cup plus 2 tablespoons butter
1¾ cups rice, cooked
¾ cup wild rice, cooked
½ cup toasted sunflower seeds (page 79)
¼ teaspoon allspice
¼ teaspoon cinnamon
4 tablespoons fresh-squeezed lemon juice
4 cups vegetable broth
1 cup white wine
1 quart jar grape leaves
Lime wedges (for garnish)
Yogurt (for garnish)

Sauté the onion, garlic, and mushrooms in 2 tablespoons butter until well browned, transfer to a medium bowl, and combine with the rice, wild rice, seeds, allspice, and cinnamon. Set aside.

In a large bowl, combine the lemon juice, broth, and wine; set aside.

Rinse the leaves to remove the brine, and place them on a work surface, shiny side down with the stem toward you. Cut off the stem, and place a tablespoon of filling in the center of the leaf. Fold the sides in toward the center, then roll it up from the stem side (think of them as tiny green burritos).

In two medium skillets, melt the remaining butter (2 tablespoons per skillet). Place the dolmas, seam side down, in the skillets, stacked tightly against each other to help keep them rolled. Add half of the liquid mixture to each skillet.

Bring to a boil, then reduce to a simmer. Cover and continue to simmer for 1 hour.

Serve hot or cold with lime wedges and a dollop of yogurt.

Oriental Salad

YIELD: 4 SERVINGS

12 ounces extra-firm tofu, cut into
1-inch cubes
½ cup teriyaki sauce
1 head lettuce
1 red pepper, diced
1 carrot, shredded
3 green onions, finely sliced
6 ounces wonton wrappers
½ cup vegetable oil
½ cup toasted sunflower seeds
(see page 79)

FOR THE DRESSING:

6 tablespoons sunflower oil
3 tablespoons rice vinegar
2 teaspoons sesame oil
2½ tablespoons teriyaki sauce
1 teaspoon hoisin sauce
2 tablespoons honey
1 teaspoon salt

Place the tofu in teriyaki sauce and let stand at least 20 minutes.

Tear lettuce into bite-sized pieces and toss with the pepper, carrot, and green onions. Set aside.

Cut the wonton wrappers into ¼-inch slices and fry them in oil in a large pan until crisp. Drain on paper towels to absorb excess oil.

Remove all but ¼ cup of the oil from the frying pan. Remove the tofu from the marinade, drain, and fry in the remaining oil for 5–10 minutes. Drain.

Mix together all seven of the dressing ingredients and pour over the salad. Add most of the wontons and all of the sunflower seeds and gently toss. Garnish with the remaining wontons.

Calabasitas

YIELD: 3 SERVINGS

2 green peppers, thinly sliced
4 small zucchini, thinly sliced
¼ pound fresh mushrooms, minced
1 tablespoon butter or margarine
¾ teaspoon salt
4 green onions, with their tops,
finely chopped
1 teaspoon red chile powder
½ pound Swiss cheese, grated
2 avocados, diced
¼ cup toasted sunflower seeds
(see page 79)
Prepared rice or corn tortillas (optional)

Lightly sauté (until al dente) the peppers, zucchini, and mushrooms in the butter or margarine. Remove from the heat and add the salt.

In a separate large bowl, gently stir the onions with the chile powder and all but 1 cup of the cheese. Add the avocado and sunflower seeds.

Stir in the sautéed pepper mixture, then sprinkle over the top the remaining cup of cheese. Serve over rice or on warmed corn tortillas.

Tabbouleh

1 head romaine lettuce, separated
into individual leaves
½ cup bulgar
3 tomatoes, finely chopped
1½ cups finely chopped parsley
¾ cup finely chopped onion
½ cup toasted sunflower seeds (page 79)
½ cup finely chopped mint

FOR THE DRESSING:

8 tablespoons olive oil
4 tablespoons lemon juice
½ teaspoon pepper or allspice
1 dash cayenne
1½ teaspoons salt

Spread the lettuce leaves on a serving platter.

Soak bulgur in hot water for 30 minutes. Drain and toss with the tomatoes, parsley, onion, seeds, and mint.

In a separate bowl, combine all of the dressing ingredients and mix well. Blend with the bulgur mixture and heap onto the centers of the leaves.

Opposite: Close-up of Mexican tithonia

Sunflower Kernel–Stuffed Mushrooms

YIELD: 4 SERVINGS

16 large mushrooms, with stems
6 tablespoons butter, softened
¼ cup toasted sunflower kernels
(page 79)
¼ cup chopped fresh parsley
1 teaspoon lemon juice
Salt to taste
Pepper to taste

Preheat the oven to 375°.

Separate the stems from the mushrooms and mince the stems. In a small bowl, mix the stems, butter, kernels, parsley, and lemon juice. Season with salt and pepper, if desired. Stuff the mixture into the mushroom heads, place them on a sheet of oiled foil, and bake for 10 minutes.

Guiltless Pesto

I think of this as guiltless because it's easier on the waistline and the pocketbook than traditional pesto, but retains a hearty flavor.

YIELD: 4 SERVINGS

2 tablespoons olive oil
4 cloves garlic, chopped
1 cup toasted sunflower seeds (page 79)
2 cups chopped fresh basil
1½ cups freshly grated Parmesan cheese
1 teaspoon salt (if your seeds are salted,
reduce to ½ teaspoon)
1 cup milk
2 tablespoons flour
3 tablespoons parsley, finely chopped

In a medium saucepan, heat the olive oil. Brown the garlic for 5 minutes, then remove it (retain the oil in the pan) and place it in a blender, along with the sunflower seeds, basil, Parmesan cheese, salt, and ½ cup milk. Blend until smooth, then set aside.

Place the flour in the pan with the oil and stir over medium-high heat for 1 minute. Add the remaining milk and stir until it begins to thicken. Add the blended mixture and continue stirring until the cheese is well melted. For a creamier pesto, you may wish to add more milk at this point. Remove from the heat and add the parsley.

Broccoli—Sunflower Stir Fry

YIELD: 4 SERVINGS

1 pound broccoli
¼ cup sunflower oil
1 eight-ounce can water chestnuts,
drained and sliced
1 teaspoon salt
½ teaspoon sugar
¼ cup water
¼ cup toasted sunflower kernels
(page 79)

Slice the broccoli stems crosswise into thin slices. Pour the oil into a wok or large frying pan, heat until sizzling, then add broccoli, water chestnuts, salt, sugar, and water. Cover and steam for about 5 minutes, stirring occasionally, until broccoli is tender. Remove from the heat, stir in the kernels, and serve immediately.

Tamari Sauté

This is tasty as a sandwich spread or as a salad dressing.

2 teaspoons sunflower oil
1 teaspoon butter
1½ cups raw sunflower seeds, hulled
3 teaspoons tamari sauce
¼ teaspoon garlic or onion powder

Melt oil and butter over medium heat in a medium-sized skillet. Add the seeds and tamari sauce and stir for 5 minutes, or until the seeds are brown. Remove from the heat and add the garlic or onion powder.

Jerusalem Artichokes and Vegetables in Herb Sauce

Courtesy of Frieda's, Inc.

YIELD: 5 SERVINGS

1 pound sunchokes
(Jerusalem artichokes), sliced
1 pound broccoli, coarsely chopped
½ pound cauliflower, coarsely chopped
⅓ cup wine
⅓ cup vegetable broth
1½ teaspoons cornstarch
2 tablespoons sliced shallots
1 tablespoon minced fresh basil
1 tablespoon minced fresh thyme
1 teaspoon Dijon-style mustard

Steam the sunchokes, broccoli, and cauliflower for 7–8 minutes. At the same time, bring the wine and broth to a boil in a small saucepan. Mix the cornstarch with 3 tablespoons of water, then add it to the saucepan. Reduce heat to medium and cook until the mixture is thickened, stirring occasionally. Remove from the heat and stir in the shallots, basil, thyme, and mustard. Transfer to a large bowl, mix with the steamed vegetables, and serve.

Light 'n' Creamy Sunchoke Soup

Courtesy of Frieda's, Inc.

YIELD: 6 SERVINGS

1 cup sliced celery
1 cup sliced onion
2 tablespoons vegetable oil
1 clove garlic, minced
2 cups chopped carrots
1 package sunchokes, scrubbed and chopped
4 cups vegetable broth
1 tablespoon lemon juice
2 tablespoons chopped parsley
1 bay leaf
1 teaspoon peppercorns
1 cup half-and-half or light cream

In a Dutch oven, sauté the celery and onion in the oil for 3 minutes. Add the garlic, carrots, sunchokes, broth, lemon juice, parsley, bay leaf, and peppercorns. Bring the mixture to a boil, then reduce to a simmer for 20 minutes, or until the vegetables are tender. Transfer the mixture to a blender or food processor and purée until smooth.

Return it to the Dutch oven, add the cream, and heat through without allowing it to boil. Serve hot.

Twig Bread

Courtesy of Gayle Ortiz of Gayle's Bakery.

YIELD: 1 THREE-POUND LOAF

FOR THE PORRIDGE:

1 ½ cups muesli
⅓ cup wheat berries
½ cup cracked wheat
½ cup rye meal (or any of the following:
pumpernickel flour, cracked rye grains,
or rye flour)
½ cup sunflower seeds
10 to 12 ounces hot water

FOR THE YEAST SPONGE:

½ cup warm water
½ teaspoon yeast
¾ cup organic (or all-purpose) white flour

FOR THE DOUGH:

1 ¾ cups organic, all-purpose flour
¾ cup organic rye flour
1 tablespoon honey
1 tablespoon sea salt
¼ cup plus 2 pinches rolled oats
1 tablespoon flax seeds
¼ to ⅓ cup water
½ cup currants
½ cup hazelnuts, toasted
½ cup sunflower seeds

In a large bowl, mix all of the porridge ingredients and allow to sit at room temperature for at least 8 hours.

For the yeast sponge, place the water in a medium bowl and sprinkle the yeast on top. Stir, then let sit for 3 or 4 minutes. Add the flour and mix until all dry spots are gone; the consistency should be like that of a thick sour cream. Let rise at room temperature at least 8 hours.

For the dough, place the white and rye flours on your work table in a mound and make a well in the middle. In the middle of the well, add the porridge and yeast sponge. Place the honey, salt, ¼ cup of oats, and flax seeds in the middle of the well also and start kneading the mixture into a dough with your hands. When all of the ingredients are well mixed, start adding the water a tablespoon at a time while continuing to knead and stretch the dough. The resulting dough should be wetter than a traditional bread dough, but not soupy.

After about 6 to 8 minutes of kneading and stretching, add the currants and hazelnuts and mix briefly to incorporate. Gather the dough into a round ball and let rise on the table or in a bowl, covered, for 45 minutes to 1 hour.

Shape the dough into a single oval loaf that will fit into a single loaf pan measuring 9 by 4½ by 3 inches. Butter the sides of the pan, then roll the loaf in the sunflower seeds and place it inside. Brush the top of the loaf with some water to keep it moist during rising and sprinkle the top with 2 pinches of oats. Let the loaf rise for 3½ hours, covered, until it rises to 1 inch above the pan.

Preheat the oven to 375°.

Bake for 1 hour 30 minutes, or until the loaf is golden brown on all sides.

Cool on a wire rack. To serve, slice very, very thin.

Cashew French Toast

From *Recipes from the Moon* by Gary Beardsworth.

This unusual French toast has a nutty, seedy taste and is vegan—it contains no egg or dairy products.

½ cup (2 ounces) cashews
¼ cup hulled sunflower seeds
¼ cup sesame seeds
1 teaspoon vanilla extract
1¼ cups plain soy milk or more, as needed
8 ounces tofu
2 tablespoons honey
½ teaspoon ground cinnamon
½ teaspoon ground nutmeg
8 slices bread of your choice,
sliced 1 inch thick

Preheat the oven to 350°.

Bake the cashews on a baking sheet for 5 minutes, or until they are lightly browned. Grind the cashews, sunflower seeds, and sesame seeds in a blender or food processor. Add all the remaining ingredients except the bread and blend, adding more soy milk if necessary to make a batter about the consistency of pancake batter. Pour the batter into a shallow dish. Dip the bread into the batter to coat both sides and cook it on a hot, oiled griddle or a hot, oiled cast-iron pan until browned on both sides. (Note: This batter is much stiffer than ordinary French toast batter. Use care when taking the bread out of the batter to keep it from tearing and falling apart.)

Aunt Madeleine's Sweet Rolls

YIELD: 12 ROLLS

¼ ounce active dry yeast
½ cup warm water
1½ cups lukewarm milk
½ cup sugar
2 teaspoons salt
2 eggs
1¼ cups butter
7½ cups flour
½ cup unsalted, toasted sunflower seeds
(page 79)
⅔ cup brown sugar
2 teaspoons cinnamon
1 cup powdered sugar
2 tablespoons milk
½ teaspoon vanilla

In a large bowl, dissolve the yeast in the water. Add milk, sugar, salt, eggs, ½ cup of the butter and 4 cups of the flour. Gradually mix in the remaining flour, one cup at a time, until the dough is soft but not sticky.

Knead the dough 5 minutes, then roll out to about 10 by 18 inches. Set aside.

For the filling, crush the sunflower seeds with a rolling pin, then toss them in a small bowl with the brown sugar and cinnamon. Melt ¼ cup of the butter and spread it on the dough. Immediately sprinkle the seed mixture on the dough.

Roll the dough into an 18-inch log and cut into 1-inch slices. Place, cut-side down, in a greased pan. Cover and let rise in a warm place for 45 minutes to 1 hour, or until doubled in bulk. Preheat the oven to 350°.

Bake the rolls for 20–25 minutes.

For the frosting, thoroughly mix the remaining ½ cup butter with the powdered sugar, milk, and vanilla. Frost the rolls while they're warm.

Choco-Dot Pumpkin Cake

YIELD: 16 SERVINGS

2 cups all-purpose flour
2 teaspoons baking powder
1 teaspoon baking soda
½ teaspoon salt
1½ teaspoons cinnamon
½ teaspoon ground cloves
¼ teaspoon allspice
¼ teaspoon ginger
1½ cups sugar
4 eggs
2 cups pumpkin
1 cup vegetable oil
1 cup semisweet chocolate chips
1 cup sunflower seeds

Preheat the oven to 350°. In a medium bowl, mix together the flour, baking powder, soda, salt, cinnamon, cloves, allspice, ginger, and sugar. Set aside.

In a large mixing bowl, beat the eggs until foamy. Add the pumpkin and vegetable oil and mix well. Add the dry ingredients, mix, and add the chocolate and seeds. Spread the mixture in a greased 10 by 4-inch pan and bake for 1 hour, or until a toothpick inserted in the center comes out clean.

Three-Seed Scones

Courtesy of Hildegard Marshall of Fatapple's
Restaurant & Bakery.

YIELD: 12 SCONES

4¼ cups all-purpose flour
1½ tablespoons baking powder
2 tablespoons sugar, plus sugar
to taste (optional)
Zest of 2 lemons
8 tablespoons butter
1 cup toasted sunflower seeds (page 79)
¼ cup poppy seeds
⅓ cup sesame seeds
5 eggs
1 cup heavy cream

Preheat the oven to 400°.

In a large bowl, mix the flour, baking powder, 2 tablespoons of sugar, and lemon zest. Cut the butter into the mixture, then blend in the sunflower, poppy, and sesame seeds. Add 4 of the eggs and the cream and stir until well blended.

Roll out the dough until it is about 1 inch thick. Beat the remaining egg, brush over the dough, and sprinkle with sugar to taste, if desired. Using a cookie cutter or knife, cut the dough into shapes and place them on a greased and floured baking sheet. Bake for 15 minutes.

Apple Sunflower Strudel

YIELD: 8 SERVINGS

1⅔ cups all-purpose flour
¼ teaspoon salt
1 tablespoon vinegar
1 egg, slightly beaten
¼ cup warm water
¼ cup white sugar
½ cup brown sugar
2 tablespoons cornstarch
1½ teaspoons cinnamon
5½ cups chopped tart apples
1½ tablespoons lemon juice
½ cup plus 2 tablespoons raw sunflower kernels
2 tablespoons plus 1 teaspoon butter
2 teaspoons honey

Preheat the oven to 400°.

In a medium bowl, mix flour, salt, vinegar, and egg. Add the water and mix. Knead until the dough is smooth. Place in a bowl, then cover and set aside 1 hour.

Mix the white and brown sugars, cornstarch, and cinnamon. On a floured pasty cloth, roll the dough into a 12 x 8-inch rectangle. Spread the apples over the dough; drizzle the lemon juice and sprinkle the sugar mixture and ½ cup of the sunflower kernels over the apples. Dot with 2 tablespoons of butter.

Using the cloth to lift the pastry, roll the dough jelly-roll fashion and seal the edges. Place on a greased cookie sheet and bake for 35 minutes.

Mix the honey and the remaining 1 teaspoon butter; spread on the crust. Sprinkle 2 tablespoons sunflower kernels over the top and bake for 10 more minutes.

Rhubarb Sunflower Loaves

YIELD: 2 LOAVES

1½ cups brown sugar
⅔ cup sunflower oil
1 egg
1 cup sour milk
1 teaspoon salt
1 teaspoon soda
1 teaspoon vanilla
2½ cups flour
1½ cups fresh diced rhubarb
½ cup toasted sunflower kernels (page 79)

FOR THE TOPPING:

½ cup sugar
¼ cup sunflower kernels
2 tablespoons butter, melted

Preheat the oven to 325°.

In the bowl of a heavy-duty mixer, thoroughly combine the first ten ingredients. Pour into two well-greased, 9 by 5-inch loaf pans and set aside.

Thoroughly mix the topping ingredients, then drizzle over the two loaves. Bake for 50 minutes.

Polenta-Millet Sunflower Bread

This is pure Americana, since sunflower seeds, millet, and corn are all native to this country. The combination of sunflower seeds and grains in this bread results in a slightly sweet, crunchy, and addictive treat.

YIELD: TWO 9 BY 5-INCH LOAVES

½ ounce active dry yeast
1 pinch sugar or a drop of honey
2¼ cups water, heated (105° to 115°)
½ cup honey
¼ cup sunflower seed oil
2 eggs
1 tablespoon salt
⅓ cup raw millet
½ cup polenta
1 cup raw sunflower seeds
2 cups whole-wheat flour
3½ to 4 cups unbleached or
all-purpose flour

In a small bowl, sprinkle the yeast and sugar or honey over ½ cup of the water. Stir to dissolve and let stand until foamy, about 10 minutes.

In a large bowl, combine the remaining 1¾ cups water, honey, oil, one of the eggs, salt, millet, polenta, ½ cup of the sunflower seeds, and whole-wheat flour. Add the yeast mixture and beat for 1 minute. Add the unbleached flour, ½ cup at a time, until a soft dough is formed that just clears the sides of the bowl. Switch to a wooden spoon when necessary if mixing by hand.

Turn the dough out onto a lightly floured work surface and knead until smooth and elastic, about 3 minutes, adding flour 1 tablespoon at a time as necessary to prevent sticking. The dough will retain a nubby, tacky quality. Place in a deep, greased container, turn once to coat the top, and cover with plastic wrap. Let rise at room temperature until doubled in bulk, about 1½ hours.

Turn the dough out onto the work surface and divide into 2 equal portions. Form into rectangular loaves and place in 2 greased 9 by 5-inch loaf pans. Cover loosely with plastic wrap and let rise at room temperature until level with the tops of the pans, about 45 minutes. Twenty minutes before baking, preheat the oven to 375°.

Beat the remaining egg and brush the tops gently. Sprinkle with the remaining ½ cup of the sunflower seeds. Bake until crusty and golden, 35 to 40 minutes. Let cool on racks to room temperature before slicing.

> *When we try to pick out anything by itself we find it hitched to everything else in the universe.*
>
> —*TEXAS BIX BENDER*

Cheesy Sun Crisps

2 cups shredded Cheddar cheese
1/2 cup grated Parmesan cheese
1/2 cup sunflower margarine, softened
3 tablespoons water
1 cup all-purpose flour
1/4 teaspoon salt
1 cup quick-cooking oats
2/3 cup toasted sunflower kernels
(page 79)

In a large mixing bowl, thoroughly blend the cheeses, margarine, and water; add flour and salt and mix well. Stir in the oats and kernels. Shape the dough into a 12-inch-long roll and wrap securely. Refrigerate for 4 hours. (The dough may be stored in the refrigerator for up to a week.)

Preheat oven to 400°. Cut the dough into 1/4-inch slices; flatten slightly. Place on a lightly greased cookie sheet and bake 8 to 10 minutes, or until the edges are a light golden brown.

Sunny Fudge

YIELD: 15 SQUARES

1 1/2 pounds peanut butter of your choice
3/4 cup honey
1 cup powdered milk
1/2 cup golden raisins
1/2 cup sunflower seeds

In a large mixing bowl, thoroughly combine all of the ingredients and spread onto an 8 by 10-inch pan. Refrigerate at least 2 hours and cut into squares.

Opposite: Russian mammoth

Granola

I have found that a few servings of this granola will satisfy a craving for less-healthy sweets. In fact, I have successfully kicked a vicious chocolate habit by substituting this granola whenever I had a chocolate craving.

YIELD: 6 CUPS

½ cup honey
½ teaspoon salt
2 cups raw oatmeal
½ cup wheat germ
½ cup sliced almonds
1 cup shredded coconut
½ cup unsalted, toasted sunflower seeds,
(page 79)
1 cup raisins

In a medium saucepan over medium heat, combine the honey and salt. Remove from the heat and transfer to a large mixing bowl, then add oatmeal, wheat germ, almonds, coconut, and sunflower seeds. Thoroughly mix and pour into a 9 by 13-inch baking pan. Bake for 10 minutes, stirring every few minutes to prevent burning, then add the raisins and bake for 10 more minutes. Again, stir frequently.

Biscotti

½ cup butter
¾ cup white sugar
3 eggs
3 cups white flour
3 teaspoons baking powder
1 cup sunflower seeds
1 ½ teaspoons vanilla

Preheat the oven to 350°

Cream the butter and sugar. Add the eggs one at a time, mixing with each addition. Add 1 cup of flour and 1 teaspoon baking powder; mix and repeat until no more remains. Add the seeds and vanilla.

Divide the dough into 3 parts. Roll and form into 3 loaves. Flatten slightly; place on cookie sheets. Bake for 20 to 25 minutes

Remove and slice into ¾-inch slices. Return these to the cookie sheets and bake another 20 minutes, or until slightly brown.

Sunny Delight

YIELD: 12 SERVINGS

3 eggs
2 cups sugar
1 cup sunflower oil
2 cups flour
1 teaspoon baking soda
2 teaspoons cinnamon
2 teaspoons vanilla
½ teaspoon salt
1 cup crushed pineapple with juice
2 cups grated carrots
½ cup shredded coconut
½ cup toasted sunflower kernels
(page 79)

FOR THE TOPPING:

½ cup shredded coconut
½ cup sunflower kernels

Preheat the oven to 350°.

Mix together the eggs, sugar, and oil. Add the flour, soda, cinnamon, vanilla, and salt. Blend in the pineapple, carrots, coconut, and kernels.

Bake for 35 to 40 minutes, or until a toothpick inserted in the center comes out clean.

For the topping, mix the shredded coconut and kernels and sprinkle over the top of the pineapple mixture as soon as it's removed from the oven.

Rainier Bars

Chewy and healthy, these bars are especially great on hiking trips—they're easy to carry and are a good source of energy.

4 cups oatmeal
2¾ cups flour
1¼ cups wheat germ
2 cups sunflower seeds
2 cups dried apricots, softened by soaking in hot water
1½ cups sunflower seed oil
½ cup dark molasses
1¼ cups honey

Preheat oven to 375°.

In a large mixing bowl, combine the oatmeal, flour, wheat germ, and seeds. Then add the remaining ingredients; mix thoroughly. Spread in a 9 by 13-inch, buttered pan and bake for 20 to 22 minutes.

Bird's Nests

This unconventional recipe was an award winner at the 1988 South Dakota state fair. Ask your kids to help out with this one—they'll love shaping the nests and filling them with M & M eggs. These make great Easter gifts, too!

YIELD: 18 COOKIES

2 cups chow mein noodles
2 cups crushed cornflakes
1 cup sunflower kernels
1 pound white almond bark
⅓ cup peanut M & Ms

In a large bowl, combine the noodles, cornflakes, and kernels; set aside. In a double boiler, melt the almond bark. Pour over the noodle mixture. To form nests, mound 2 tablespoons of the mixture on a cookie sheet and make indentations in the center. Allow to set at room temperature, then add the M & M "eggs."

Sunseed Toffee Bars

YIELD: 15 BARS

⅓ cup salted, toasted sunflower kernels
(see page 79)
¼ cup sunflower oil margarine, chilled
½ cup brown sugar
1 egg yolk
½ teaspoon vanilla
1 cup all-purpose flour
⅛ teaspoon salt
1 cup semisweet chocolate chips

Preheat the oven to 350°.

Blend the sunflower kernels in a food processor until a paste forms. Cut the margarine into pieces and add it to the processor along with the sugar, egg yolk, and vanilla. Process until smooth, 10 to 15 seconds. Add the flour and salt and process another 10 seconds, until well blended.

Place the mixture in a lightly greased, 9 by 13-inch pan and bake 12 to 15 minutes, or until the edges are lightly browned. Immediately sprinkle with chocolate chips and return the pan to the oven until the chips are soft.

When cool, cut the bars and refrigerate to set the chocolate.

Pudding for Birds

If you live in an area that has cold winters, the birds in your backyard may appreciate this treat. An ideal method of feeding is to dig holes in a small log and stuff the holes with the pudding.

YIELD: 2 QUARTS

3½ cups water
2 cups cornmeal
1 cup peanut butter
¾ cup sugar
1 cup black ("oil") sunflower seeds
(available in many garden centers)

Bring the water to a boil, then add the cornmeal and reduce the heat to low. Stir until thick. Remove from the heat and add the peanut butter, sugar, and seeds.

Unused portions can be kept in the refrigerator for up to a month.

BIRD TREAT

Pick a large sunflower head and bore a small hole through the top. Attach a wire long enough to twist around a tree branch. Lightly coat the face of the sunflower with peanut butter, and hang it from a tree branch. You'll be surprised by the amount of avian interest this will generate!

Bird Seed Treat

The black sunflower seeds used in this recipe have a high oil content and are by themselves a great food source for birds. But I like to give birds a bit more variety, and have found that many species enjoy the following mixture.

YIELD: 2½ QUARTS

4 cups black sunflower seeds
2 cups millet seeds
2 cups peanuts
2 cups raisins or dried berries
1 cup thistle

*T*he flowers
of all the
tomorrows are
in the seeds
of today.

—CHINESE PROVERB

*Deep in
their roots,
all flowers
keep the light.*

—*THEODORE
ROETHKE*

Seed Sources

ARIZONA
Native Seeds/SEARCH
2509 N. Campbell Ave.
Tucson, AZ 85719
(520) 327-9123

CANADA
William Dam Seeds
P.O. Box 8400
Dundas, ON
Canada L9H 6M1

COLORADO
Lake Valley Seed
5717 Arapahoe
Boulder, CO 80303
(800) 333-4882

KENTUCKY
Shooting Star Nurseries
444 Bates Road
Frankfort, KY 40601
(502) 223-1679

MAINE
Johnny's Selected Seeds
Foss Hill Road
Albion, ME 04910
(207) 437-4301

MINNESOTA
Prairie Moon Nursery
Route 2, Box 163
Winona, MN 55987
(507) 452-1362

NEW MEXICO
Seeds of Change, Inc.
P.O. Box 15700
Santa Fe, NM 87506
(800) 957-3337

NORTH CAROLINA
Niche Gardens
1111 Dawson Road
Chapel Hill, NC 27516
(919) 967-0078

OREGON
Territorial Seed Co.
Box 157
Cottage Grove, OR 97424
(541) 942-9547

PENNSYLVANIA
W. Atlee Burpee Co.
300 Park Ave.
Warminster, PA 18974
(800) 888-1447

SOUTH CAROLINA
Park Seed Co.
Cokesbury Road
Greenwood, SC 29647
(800) 845-3369

SOUTH DAKOTA
Gurney's Seed & Nursery Co.
110 Capital Street
Yankton, SD 57079
(605) 665-1671

VERMONT
The Cook's Garden
P.O. Box 53528
Londonderry, VT 05148
(802) 824-3400

VIRGINIA
Southern Exposure
Seed Exchange
P.O. Box 170
Earlysville, VA 22936
(804) 973-4703

WISCONSIN
Prairie Nursery
P.O. Box 306
Westfield, WI 53964
(608) 296-3679

Prairie Ridge Nursery
9738 Overland Road
Mt. Horeb, WI 53572
(608) 437-5245

The **National Sunflower Association** is a great source of information about sunflowers:
4023 State St.
Bismark, ND 58501
(701) 328-5100

Suggested Reading

Buchanan, Carol. *Brother Crow, Sister Corn.* Berkeley, California: Ten Speed Press, 1991.

Heiser, Charles B. *The Sunflower.* Norman, Oklahoma: University of Oklahoma Press, 1976.

Morse, Kitty. *Edible Flowers.* Berkeley, California: Ten Speed Press, 1995.

Poncavage, Joanna. *Totally Sunflowers.* Berkeley, California: Celestial Arts, 1996.

Sitton, Diane Morey. *Sunflowers.* Layton, Utah: Gibbs Smith, 1995.

Squire, David. *The Gardener's Guide.* London: Salamander Books Ltd., 1991.

Wilson, Gilbert L. *Buffalo Bird Woman's Garden.* St. Paul, Minnesota: Minnesota Historical Society Press, 1987.

Index

Also by Barbara Flores

These framing-quality posters are a beautiful addition to any wall—kitchen, greenhouse, bedroom, or office. The larger poster measures 24 x 36, and the thinner one measures 12 x 36.

Other "Great" books in this series include: *The Great Chile Book* and *The Great Salsa Book*, by Mark Miller and John Harrison; *The Great Citrus Book*, by Allen Susser; *The Great Exotic Fruit Book*, by Norman van Aken and John Harrison; *The Great Hot Sauce Book* and *The Great American Microbrewery Beer Book*, by Jennifer Trainer Thompson; and *Ken Hom's Asian Ingredients*, by Ken Hom.

For more information, or to order, call us at the number below. We accept VISA, Mastercard, and American Express. You may also wish to write for our free catalog of over 500 books, posters, and audiotapes.

TEN SPEED PRESS / CELESTIAL ARTS

(800) 841-BOOK

P.O. Box 7123, Berkeley, CA 94707